The Gate

THE GATE

poems

ﾃ

William H. Lewis

The Pelican Press • Albion, California • 2014

ᘓ

Front Cover Painting "The Gate" by William H. Lewis
Back Cover Painting "Love in the Grass" by William H. Lewis

There's a lot of them, throughout our small jurisdiction,
inspired thoughts and flowers I mean.

CB

Thank you Karen

Table of Contents

Covenant

Everything else now I see, moves with grace, or not at all.
A perfect calm, not like our minds which race to keep up
with one another in the absence of reckless words.

Everything else now, has recognized its own disarray,
and seems to be comfortable with it.

Not like us whose convulsions of thought have tumbled through
the corridors, colliding with an inevitability,
oh so imminent.

I mean, I've heard of love that leans like twin aspens in
a binding covenant.
Everything else now is covered with a brilliant white cape
that appears to covet silence, demand it.

Steep grottos of darkened stone usher cascades' slow motion.
In the distance, your breathing too seems far away,
as if I could begin again without you being aware of it.

I clench the edge of morning, not wanting to sense the perfume
of its departure.

And you, the enigma, drifting with me,
the possession of our affection held close, like a precious
amulet, fastened through our bodies, and into our souls.

It turns out that nothing can mend our fragility.
Lamenting only bends under its own weight, sending us out
looking for another passage.

Convincing Me About Her

To her chest is open, open to the birds of weaving,
guides to proximity's weakest care.

She'll have lit the walls with shadow, which cannot
be made to define her, her measuring devices and shit
like that, that deserve attention,

if only that.

Where does a winding wish take me far, and far away
from her, and the quiet sorting of things about her that
we may find interesting, like

what does she do for inspiration, when the bluest blue,
lies beyond precious,

ribbons tied with sun flair, and openings shifting shine?

ℭ

Navarro Ridge

Pearl of the Sea

I long for the purity of rock meeting water,
green shrouded countenance, struggling beauty that can dissolve
like an icon cast in salt.

I have preserved nature's shimmering evanescent rumors, keenly in
the past, far from cold reaching fingers.
Far from the terrible beauty that mocks all who aspire to be like it,
mindless, deadly.

The clap of physics all around.

What a fine race of beings some have become, all clean, not hungry,
modern fighters searching for other primitive minds to slay,
a grave hoax smoking scrolls away.

Each stalk of sea-borne kelp trembles in finite exhalations.
Nostrils wounded, poor man here,
straying for awhile, lost in this temporal jungle.

In simple arrogance, beasts crouch, hissing fragments, uncoiling
menace lit by beach fires, fanned in a husky salt-soaked voice.

It is not just that I love the oyster,
mortals can seldom fathom capricious love,
but the gods know it to be the pearl of the sea.

Remembrance

Sometimes I brush by, standing in a different place,
sensing a fragrance, or sound,
feeling its moment of importance.

The birthstones of providence seem to melt
as the years thunder by.

I cannot possibly decipher all that becomes lost,
as shadows reach across that rash of luminescence
that tries to light my way.

ଔ

Justin's Birthday
Big Sur

The Faint Scent of Love

I still come here, my life permits it.
This ground so sacred,
this air, pure as the wish of a child.

These massive swells are like slow moving tongues,
tasting ever higher on the beach,
reaching out to see if the Earth has begun to heal herself

and then retreating.

Leaving the trilliums' minute souls uncounted,
and stream's serpentine way about her,
as she descends into a cool blue womb of her own.

I know that from this distance I am tasting
just the faint scent of love,
but it is enough to entice me.

I know that it is blown off course many times
on its way here, by the far away celestial storms,
then Earth's temporal pull,

and we have never known how to treat it,
when it finally arrives.

Truth

Truth becomes the changing tool. I also mean
the place of strident choices, blooms of clocks'
brash minutes.

Hunting others relies on day's honest light,
in other words: the symmetry of physics.

Getting a deluge of sand in my cuffs, running the dunes again,
becoming feverish and dark in the shadow of a fixed sigh.

I wish now for the ache of familiarity, through hardened
capillaries: women, men, sisters and brothers, predators.

Truth is the clay this morning was groomed for,
yet it wanders as a new river seeking the sea.

It can be heavy like clay, its potential left in a
plastic bag somewhere,
hardened, as if it was not on time to greet the rain.

Running Man

Red hunting lodge on an escarpment overlooking an estuary,
moving in enormous circles of hemorrhaged nostalgia.

Layers of forest do not respond beyond a natural dignity,
an unflinching serenity, that can be traced as far as the back
of the canyon where sleeping huts float in terminal sin flare.

The paths between them, busy with coffee-drinking young men
and women, skirting ankle high hedges. Their children have accepted
that they are simply the chemistry of erratic couplings,
left in fitful sleep.

Fog becomes the boundary of their dreams, lost in inertia,
lost in the dark myth about them.

The green shades to a black corner, a voice, "You can be here,
but you must slice and cut with us,
surrender with us to peace anxiety, vow to return
to a fighting stance."

All this time, I have been trying to keep pace with a running man,
who has tripped on the hedges, unaware that he had become
lethal in his senseless, billowing years.

03

Inn at the Market, Seattle

Perfect Astonishment

I've rinsed my thoughts over and over, wishing to cleanse them,
that woman #1 can barely wish away, by clicking her tongue.

Bereft.

Along all the ridges, high above the blue of the Mediterranean Iris,
whipped to shreds below Mistral's power and loveliness.

I am, wherever simple, one last shriek in the tree shore and shallows,
learning to weigh loss, as it might seek the nostalgia of a natural
commons.

I am without power too, standing in wind's open arms, motionless,
unable to hold for long that grip of ascent, locked and spinning,
moving easily above shrines woven with new grace.

 Always it seems, flooding to the brim of haste, filled with perfect
astonishment, as graceful water has fallen to time and passage.

There is a drift of rock in the mind-hewn shore, where mystic orators
have fumed, ranted, and quelled with logic, man's words,
man's lonely words.

You can never see once walls have been built, every summer
mortar and rock extinguishing insight, I wish you a blessing, driver of
salt spray lesson's sad flower, still clinging to the memory of your sun.

This maddened howl, a crazed Adam, and his Eves, and their scrappy family's burnished light, amidst the raw intermittent tones of forgiveness.

ೞ

Looking between the trees

Crabs

The skeletal crabs that support the weight of the deep
alloyed sun water, always move sideways along
contours of feigned indifference.

Their fierce hard eyes constantly record what is going on
beyond those contours.
Piercing scribes play at breaching them,
yet seldom do they lurch forward to explore another's.

Yes, crabs do covet what they sense they will never taste,
and seldom knowingly disrupt the powerful tide of
crab etiquette, subject to the pressure of the deep
and sparse bottom.

Translations of their chattering, unintelligible language
do not exist. Higher thinkers seem apathetic,
lesser thinkers really only like to eat them, feel soft white
unprotected flesh roll softly in their cheeks.

Impatience treats all unfathomable territory with the same
Indifference, that is why the sun reaches way down to nourish
their tiny brains,

but it may just as well be rivers of crab food,

gone dry.

Two Men

In the middle of a parking lot, a man goes to his car,
and lights it up.

The wheels will not turn, rubber and asphalt have become one.

The man returns to his office.

He sinks his teeth into his duties, one day ahead.

The man's friend goes to the car, and commands it to move.

It rolls ahead freely, leaving the car and his friend to return
again to his room, where he listens excitedly to news
that is one day early.

But there is a painting close to the door he uses to go and come,

with sounds of contentment looking his way, although he
knows that happiness most always turns, and is gone,

or becomes just another pixel pastel.

Paintings

Paintings warn the way people rush,
so it might be less likely to heel to the artist shorn of her capacity.

Within shore bed chaparral, my long time friend emerges,
standing in the shadows of falling shards, dark Welsh slate.

Dazzled by the tendencies that move within that silent place,
amidst newly discovered divergence.

Who would want to possess a painting whose creator restrained
her joy, kept her sorrow sent away.

The blaze of sun falters, never to watch the mane of a breaking swell
veer off to the south,
never to reach up to touch the rain, the heat in mountains bring.

Out of darkness, sleep stays tucked under its embrace,
entering the house of philosophy with a shattered roof,
shimmering on the bluff,

overlooking interminable lines, and lines of jagged sea foam,
becoming lost in the thickness of a darkened impasto,
making the canvas heavy,

making it difficult to choose which frame to build.

Over the years they come, altering the fixed nature of the house,
making it lighter, more vulnerable to summer gales,
less able to become a painting, more like a charcoal sketch,
blown to enter the Earth and say, "I am here."

Another life, another empty frame, another dwelling place
to thicken the circumference of this.

&

Paradise, Mt. Rainier

Purpose

The germ of spirit fusion can be the vicious thought
held back, drowned in a solution of restraint and living air.

Restraint is the first sign of life, and purpose without a canopy
of the divine has no ideas worthy of the fragile
wings of a poet.

If you are gentle with your view of the core of this world,
and trust in the decline of rage,

wish for delicacy within your part in the paradox of God,
and the vocation of love.

Perhaps you will choose not to lie back and watch from your
guarded place, celestial bodies wander across the sky,

but learn from the stumbling person where not to step, and
how to die.

ഷ

Pilar's

The Levant

It is the hushed clarity melting hue to blue, just nimble swims
new waxy stitch, left to float in a small sea, out on a leaf,

influenced by the strength of the Levant, yet drifting to west,
not realizing the cadence of an acceptable pause.

Trapped in parentheses, trapped in the current that becomes the
West, with all of the themes and expectations of it.

Becoming homesick for the Levant. Parting the cool blue waters,
doing the breast stroke, I can see the coast of Spain, the mirage
of North Africa.

I attach myself to a powerful barge, with three butterfly motors
greaseless and clean, overcoming currents, blasting
toward the Strait.

I slowly return, but the butterflies will not eat, cannot graze the
garden's bright offerings, colors fade, life itself fades.

With the ebb, the barge turns listlessly in the calm sea.

I speak of endings less and less, pale structures of feeble energy,
and the names I thought I would never forget,
softly forgotten.

Trains

Now a long train which becomes just two engaged engines,
channeling strength through one another, with no cars to pull.

Standing knee-deep in winter's pensive graffiti,
I am thinking about my eighth grade teacher, Sister Agnes Claire

at St. Finbar School,
where the boys wore grey uniforms and maroon ties.

Sister loved me, and in my own simple way, I loved her.
She taught me that love can happen out of family, and between
the most unlikely people.

And Reeva, the blond saint from Avalon, strong, tied to the Earth—
She taught me that certain drugs can play a profound
and provocative part in growing up.

They can forgive us our trespasses and lighten our hearts into
the deepest places.

She taught me that I should never think that I really know
another person, and that I should always be open to the reality of
surprise. Yes I can learn; I will never stop learning.

Reeva could play pool, both barroom Nine Ball, and sophisticated
Billiards, if she wanted.
She could consistently, and playfully beat me, if she wanted.

I learned all this, that night at the Isthmus.

What else did I not know about Reeva? This was just the start of my
not knowing about Reeva, and everything else in this world.

I think–but do not know –that there are spring flowers under this snow,
waiting to reach into the sky for their God,

and that the fire and smoke I see, coming from the distance will stop,
and the cold crisp snowy world of late winter,
and the two engines with no cars to pull
will soon be on their way.

C3

Two Harbors

In the Eyes of a Mirror

This body,
a tool designed for the most profound intercourse.

This mind,
a most delicate mosaic,
watched over by an angel, whose softest wishes
become my illusive intuition,
though I must continue to live within the shadow
of my own mortality,

so long it has taken me to be here now,
looking into the eyes of a mirror.

Slender Girls

I can't tell if the pace is right.
I don't look around for the guide that guides others now,

for a light to walk or run by,
taste your lust and mine by.

A narrow, concrete trough to bathe my feet in,
to soften my thoughts in.

Listen, your ears were made for this, hold still
while numbness crushes,
and statistics sell themselves in coded display,

while I lay parallel to the ones who have fallen and loved,
but cannot go on.

They have felt guilt, just as I have, so what makes us different,
here on the hot ground, in the moonlight?

I cannot see their faces, the faces of feigned tolerance.
Go on, rip the shell apart, tear a simple ripeness
before the snare becomes impotent.

I will not keep the slender girls away, only wishing
I could hardly see them,

hardly make sense of them at all.

&

West Point Inn, Mt. Tamalpais

Not Free to Die

We are not free here, our wisdom has become sterile,
fractured by the poles,
visiting revelations, warily out of reach.

I can only know that celestial horizons' many stars,
seem to be seeking anonymity.

I can see them fade into the slate grey waterway,
its darkening form slowly moving into a frightening propensity.

I will touch with my fingers the open wound, I will feel the heat, the
sanguine reality, becoming immune to the scent of divinity.

Son of Man

I love this man, who I only know about through
other men's writings, which have become aged paintings in my mind.

Pictures that I am at peace with, images that have become
comfortable, yet have little authority over the concepts of others.

I propose that this life invokes obscurity, I feel this, as I descend
the stairs of thought, down into a forest, dark with unsound reasoning.

The words of men float through.

Unable to stop them, I made up my own, soon coagulating
Into poems, laments, entreaties.

Merging together, all the words become indistinguishable and lonely,
amidst meager accomplishments that cause grief
for the sins that were committed in their honor.

I could hold onto truth like a sacred dove, but I must hold on tight, or
it will fly away, into a sky thick with other doves that have flown away,

lost in the darkest of clouds.

Looking Down

I always look down on this cove,
the cliffs are way too dangerous, so I stay on the grassy amphitheater
high above crystal depth and agitated shallows.

Up here around me, the months trade sensations, and
the shadows of their passing become a blur of emotions.

Lately when I stay on into early evening, Venus rules the sky,
making vast suns beyond seem dim in comparison.

I love the work of time, the pace and embrace of it,

but I cannot stay forever here on this bluff, looking into another
world, where submerged lovers hold on tight, never let go,
and do not glance up at me through darkening water,
or beckon me to join them.

Venus is lighting up my only world now, and she seems to be softly
floating away.

In the Air We Breathe

Time is old, it filters through delicate leaves and becomes the
air that nourishes this blue planet.

Now disguised, holding its breath for the young ones.

Seasons fly apart with time that has no boundaries,
yet remembers all the renovations,

and chronicles man's constant contradictions
to the flow of love,

where his tools never could find the delicacy he has yearned
for, outside the garden he knows is there.

ଦ

Cafe Kevah, Big Sur

Debris

Cities blister my eyes,

chisel my thoughts, crusting along seams of bright intentions,
small brittle pieces of syntax break off, drift to relocate themselves,

then dive and disappear into the universal gyre,
where they spiral into that rusted galaxy, harmfully close.

What embodiment can toy with our earth-bound thoughts, adjust them
into what appears to be just another destroyer, quiet as ice,
yet symmetrically magnificent as a snowflake?

As I have grown more and more vindictive, missing
the answer, nothing has changed.

Men still grip at what they have imagined to be enlightenment, and
usually settle for shallow vocations, easily picked.

Gossiping intellects, weeds in a garden that could have been,
only nourished by incessant blood and tears,
no rain from the heavens,
no jade carvings in the looming refuse pile,

that only grows and grows into the silhouette of a mountain that
no one wants to climb.

ఔ

Queenie's

Always Find Love Alone

I used to fight for pensive thoughts, among frenzied upward steps,
wishing to be lost in caravans of tiny bubbles, safe in the body of
them, held for awhile by praying ferns, turning in lazy half circles.

Here is this fanfare of light upon meandering coils, superb inverted
hearts of green.

Not a gesture or shimmering fragment's breath can touch the notes, as
if they were ivory keys, segments of a blossom's white body,
waiting to be rearranged by vanquished harm's most powerful quiet.

Touching all manner still to tarry, hesitant swans of light
regally emerging, held in dappled ferns' array.

And in that, in brooks shallowest most intrepid flow, how else, floating
favors beg, to always find love alone, without whispers, crying or sin.

03

Botanical Gardens, Brook Trail

Three Pools

We float above the dunes,

perceiving our view of emerald water through a crown
of palm fronds, gently stirring up the shadows.

Truth, cruelty, and sensuality have drained into separate pools,
ours to bathe in as we wish.

You have chosen the pool of truth, where kaleidoscopes
of sun-bleached trash line its shore.

Flowers of plastic that have earned the right to lie, like pastel
jewels, where lament drips slowly into the sand.

I have chosen the pool of sensuality, a deeper pool,
clear, yet with an uncertain bottom.

I look for You

I see your desk, your computer, the window looking
out on meadows and redwoods.

With you not there, what would be the purpose of my life?

It is you who has brought me through the desert of obscurity,
through the color of regret.

I view the summer equinox, the heat of June,
through love's gentle prism.

I sense the coming of a simple philosophy, but I'm not there.
You glance up and smile.

Looking at you is like seeing my first planet without a telescope,
giving when I am in no mood to give,

dancing with strangers that are surely you.

CB

For Karen

Autumn in Vermont

After a flake of snow passed the depths of heaven,
it landed on my eyelid and softly melted into a tear,
I quickly wiped it away.

This fading crimson in Vermont, a taste of the passage of time,
a prayer for a vestige of faith.

The last swarm, leaves lie bare, skeletons
for winter, the thief of warmth,

yet inside though, coals glow like the eyes of a dragon.

Where Campfires Burn

The tides of May find soft places to purge the senses,
clasp an evening's mood and sail away.

The osprey moves in among bright curls of perfumed thermals;
she rests on them for a moment,

tasting the wet tangy salt of her last dive.

Dark banks of razor muscles open and become one with the flowing
surge of full moon's drifting silver river.

The inlet rich with crimson lichen,
blackened rock where campfires burn, and wild stories float
for awhile, before joining quiet bones below.

Everything human, bent or severed by weeping, seagoing angels.
Everything human, poignant, forgotten in the time it takes

to find another prayer to send aloft.

Nepenthe Morning

Impossible patterns of brilliant crushed diamonds
in the midst of a vast pool of sleeping mist,

born in the blue watersheds of those lofty sentinels,
where color has anointed the upward meadows,

chiseling new facets, reaching, and giving way
only to the flow of love.

ᄻ

Nepenthe: The potion in Homer's Odyssey that
banished grief and trouble from a person's mind.

Banished

All too seldom echoes grow, crowds lie abandoned,
low, under spans of holding roots.

Sepia turnstiles churn a froth of talented virgin housewives,
never scrubbing again those kitchen sinks, the white ones,

as pure as ocean foam against black volcanic sand.
This wet scent, our dearest faded veil, heralded
in passion and simplicity.

Looking keenly into any long pause presents a procession
of constricted urgency.

These chords of thought can sting like a cornered lie,
and form grey mist, profound yet incomplete,
tasteless yet pungent.

Always passing through the years of hunched-over meridians,
meaningless travel, although each step had its own dream.

So much so that it could have been gone, and gone and gone.

As sentry, I have had clarity and upward sight,
I have become a winner, where nothing is ever contested,

nothing floats that will not sink, nothing brought along
that will not make a shadow.

❡

In the Botanical Gardens

The Wild Young Ones

I can look up and see the wild young ones dancing, offering
themselves to the moment.

They don't care to look into the future, at least
not until their mood has passed.

Then they will smash the uneasiness of restraint.
They will join the water birds, when the moon has lost her lucent way.

They will change their plumage, fragrance, proximity,
and their philosophy.

Human boundaries mean nothing to them.

Squelched

This winter's night, all of my dreamy thoughts have congealed into
ethereal actors and actresses, relentless and unfulfilled.

They line up into veins of pulsing energy, wanting to become alive.

Spitting coals and ultimatums like brazen children,
no concept of the futility of emptiness.

Meteors that long to reach the Earth,
burned in their hapless trajectories.

Squelched by the frost that paints the meadows white.

As Friendship Fades

You made up a rhyme this morning to suit yourself.
With its blend of fetters and glimpses beyond your natural way,

and for every leaf that falls within your small realm,
another thought is born, bristling away our sweet bond.

While you were in your bath, I stood by the open door of your closet.

The fragrance from your clothes made my presence there
seem as an intrusion,

as if I were standing in a story buried within
the locked pages of your diary.

It is time, I think, to weep for those lost days of emerald pools,
glistening sand crystals, and skies lit by Venus.

I fear a lee shore now,
a harbor shallow and opaque with sorrow.
This day and your poem, borne along with the current.

I lie alone as friendship fades, our bodies entwined in need.

Geckos race among the rafters,
beckoning us to join their reckless play.

My Yawl

Once aboard my yawl, I was making up lines,
enjoying our resting moments tied to the Earth.

My yawl is a lovely lady down wind,
her sails set scooping up the breeze.

Her gaff rig, archaic, so she doesn't point well,
but I am in no hurry,

now that the blisters on my hands
have long since disappeared.

ဆ

Cat. Harbor, Isthmus

Heart's Grove

Intention's white fog catches defeated judgment, here
the wishbone among spores and drifting lungs, shade
broken with bunches of spotted light.

There would only be the sound of a drifting edge,
this swan had so deep her magnificence shown, as
something else known or just revealed,

needing darkness to forgive her unearthly white
needing a lord within her heart to sweep mountains'
ashes into a promised delay of touches,

within heart's grove of wishes.

A disk of unfolding flags swings by, showing my beginning
and beguiling end, but only with eyes I trade among others.

Leaving my scent upon the lavender, hoping it would
become familiar, like the concept of futility.

I've sensed the beauty rise like a beauty unknown, it
Is within my suspended mind, only there that I can see
and swim through perfumed air.

Eyes of Evolution

One would think that we are all the same, inside I mean.
Look if you could, at the heart of a long distance runner,
a lover, a saint.

If you could look inside a soul though, you might see a beautiful
void, a poetry book waiting for its poems,
a sunset waiting for its sun,

a child, waiting for her father.

You might see language waiting to be translated,
soft and sweet as syrup running down the maple
in clumsy abundance.

You might see the dark potential of evil puddling in the corner,
searching for its catalyst.

You might see a vast reach of nothingness, waiting for the flight of
the red tail, or not.

But you would see through the eyes of evolution, so all real
potential would be hidden, or perhaps if the angels willed it so,
a gesture of the brilliance

that is yet to come.

ଔ

West Point Inn, Mt. Tamalpais

Places I Want to Be

Hapless thoughts, notes of time, written, translated,
sent into the screeching summer doldrums, rubbing
sores and half-healed insults,
that thaw the ice of indifference with a certain
paradoxical tenderness.

If I had a heart that could taste remorse, I could rest,
instead of flying along the tarmac, shaving sparks from my spine,
screaming at injustice as it glides by.

Even though airports leave me partially paralyzed,
they do bring me to places I want to be,
sailing in the sky past seashells I will never see.

The Universe Is Ours

I love you. Those words so often spoke.
As humbling as the need for bread and air,
to surrender your lips and soul together.
Holding dear the temple of trust.

Everything in this moment glides by the open space.
The wings of angels, disassembled, left to drift on their own.
The holy ones, brought down by the gravity we all must share.

Here we are, the corridors are full, the campsites taken.
I look for my reflection in a store window, just to make sure I still exist.

It's true, my love, after begging for a moment,
the universe is ours.

CB

Early Bakery, with Katherine

Glow of an Angel's Wings

She first noticed sin in her early teens, although it was just the
concept, just the silent unfolding of it, from where it came,
she was not sure.

At times it made her shoulders sore.
It wasn't until her landscape became unfamiliar,
that she looked directly into sin.

It was then that she felt the strong sinew and
new feathers push through.
Her time body mixed with an ethereal form, brilliant
shimmering light.

She became an angel, or rather, she was an angel all along,
its just that her loving nature acquired a guide,
and her new wings were resplendent, and were not just for show.

She could fly.

In that moment, a billion years of crying, but not seeing,
so many illusions, hidden in assumptions.

Her sweet soul read the letters, before the meadow flowers
choked up with time—less spent—could say.

To rest she merged with deepening fallen blossoms that shared with a drifting sentiment, their lovely essence.

Be done with sin.

This is how this planet will become a radiant force among the stars.

Poison Fuels Evil

En el sur,
simply a bleached shell, cast up upon the dune,
where wands of sea grass trace glyphs,
inspired by the capricious wind.

En el norte
The years melt away as spring hail does.
Poison fuels evil, in the bay you can see the sea
trying to cleanse the part it cannot reach.

Where the mad chatter of divisive humanity
is scratching away at a noble world.

Strangers

They are always around me, in the night, and in the day,
in my dreams they confront me.

When they come near, their energy pervades the thin shroud of grace
that I have summoned to protect me.

Some come as messengers, with news that will always benefit them,
and drain my thinking down to anguish.

Some come as bright spirits, that could merge into my life.
How can I ever tell who is who, disguised as they are,
all speaking around and around, seldom giving their hand?

Afraid as I have become.

C8

Isthmus, Catalina Island

Riddles

Shells turn to white powder,
our moon is a crescent of light.
The axe has an arch of power,

and in the air we breathe, riddles swim as schools of silvery fish,
turning into each other and joining in strength,
columns of menace so frail.

Sometimes I think we were not meant to skip along
the surface of the sea, its bottom deep and
rugged, below us, waiting.

We can build like frenzied architects, bruised by our endeavors,
but always we return and spread our arms into the crystals
that are life and hope.

And again, into that white powder, not yet stained,
lying quietly beneath the sun.

CB

Bahía de Los Angeles

Love

I dove ahead, better than I would have
among recognized paradigms.

I may seem to reappear, moving past cast retention,
floating in the lingering of breath and wishes.

All of the elements believe in physics.
Their God in time puts blossoms where the sun has been,
sure of its return,

lets love go its special way, unencumbered by logic.
A brief, yet potent, visitor though.

Horizon to Horizon

Kelp forests acquiesce their lover's grip upon the rocks
sensing storm's command,
sacrificing themselves upon the shore.

Horizon to horizon, our star lowers
her veil of dazzling light,
nourishing azure gardens below.

Descending buttresses of green-shrouded stone and
the blackest earth have swallowed summer's inferno.
The condor quietly spirals to his lofty tabernacle.

And below, just as the tiny refracted glint of an ant wandering
across the crown of a skull,
one of our souls reflects her new light upward.

To her, death is simply the taking away of gravity.
God has saved this morning's grace for her.

CB

Nepenthe, Big Sur

What Monarchs Seek

Few of us have a taste for just the sun alone.

So many travel to find their eyes diverted onto nocturnal fields,
where planets' dimness has traveled so far to reach.

Others sound, tasting what their eyes cannot see.

They have forsaken the sun,
even though it is the sun that monarchs seek.

Lilting through the pungent eucalyptus canopy
leading down to the tormented sea.

CB

Andrew Molera, Big Sur

Golden Gate

This Golden Gate sentinel ushers swift ocean currents.
I stand on cold painted steel, looking down.

Thinking of all the haunting moods
water has offered me throughout my life.

Legions of lycra-clad cyclists advance,
each one a different circuit in an immense breaker box,

switched on.

ନ୍ଦ

West Point Inn, Mt. Tamalpais

Throwaway Memories

Remember how a crumb falls, telling us of its slight journey,
and how the thickness of the air cuts the noise of its descent
for a time, forgetting loaves arranged to sell.

Remember how the celestial equator drifts overhead, and will
separate us, show us the magic of rivers' seasonal slumber
and winter privilege, cry for our fall into this den of lions.

We must learn to listen to their rage within a certain time.
Put the influenced air between us,
make me sure that this wind-blown rain
can dissolve the sculpted dunes.

It is quite another secret now, hiding among bluish mountains.
Teacher, student, guardian—I can't tell, it all becomes
heartaches interwoven, full of mercy, abandon, and silence.

I shall split the day once again, becoming present in time,
and then lost in thought,
harvesting small bits of wisdom among throwaway memories.

This Notion

My will, I hope, will never vary.

My hope, I hope, will never cease.

Although trees seem to pray to an empty sky,
it is there, cold and deep in dark array.

The newest kindness already has a family that loves it.

Time, now a wide caress, just became morning,
with drops of a wet night, still lingering on its leaves.

I sense a sadness here on this world, swimming
through channels of light, yet far, far away,
and all around.

This notion—that man should not hurt his fellow beings—
comes from the future, not the past, not searching
our memories' flow of tears.

It comes from the divine plan of the cosmos.

It comes from the yearning of a student.

It comes from her asymmetrical thoughts.

It comes from his theory of spiritual colors.

It comes from within the gates of wisdom.

It comes from our children's future suffering,
long after our counted breaths subside.

Transgressions

I live within a pond of kindness.

Around its edges bulbs spring forth, as clouds make
cylindrical passage,
heating and cooling a tarnished bowl, half buried in the bank.

I live within a capricious mirror, clearly lit when stillness insists.

But when I run truant from forms and clarity,
with transgressions small and large,

only affection follows, with inquisitive fragrances that
transcend the moment,
their smoky voices close to water's lapping coil.

Morning

In splendid morning man is quiet.

Monoliths sparkle, reaching to gather and assemble
slivers of new light.

Farther out, tragic mist wanted to move forward,
but the green sun was there, holding on to its deepest places.

Now, burnished outcroppings feel the pull of ill-choice.

On and on we sleep, awakened only by blow of ax.
Cliffs, long, blue, and filmy, slide along the horizon.
How much more to take? Immense, tireless propensities here,

shrunken, to precisely the size we love,

held as a finite yet menacing fist.
Held steady, as the cosmos wields her swinging mantle.

Some feel lost, walking among death's early needs,
tripping on the shade of morning's invisible roots.

Parson's Landing

Pixilated

His yawl, up on blocks, with a good view of the estuary, has
left him standing alone on the mossy dock.

Only on the sea does he not
have to choose which mask to wear.

He glances up.

His head and neck have become pixilated,
and seem to be drifting with the current.

One Day We Shall Die My Love

A southern latitude, a sandy spit dividing an estuary,

I met a woman.

Her body reminded me of the dunes that looked down on us.

Before I met her, I wanted to sail more that day, and
climb deeply into the rocks.

I never thought what to do with love I
couldn't dash away from.

We stood together, a strange dream forming around us,

with tastes of sea creatures that spiral out of reach, into
turquoise water as we approach.

She turned to me and whispered,
"One day we shall die my love, but not before we have lived."

CȜ

Isla Espíritu Santo

The Pond

The ship came close, loaded deep.
Many cars waited, and worried, hoping to receive
their allotment of cubes.

It looked like it was too much for the small dock,
the pond was overflowing, the wind seemed desperate,

taking in large and small breaths that had nothing to do
with corrosion, and how it could creep back into its place
in the bank, where stranded mud hens patiently wait.

The ship rested, tied securely to the dock.
Inside the dissimilar cubes there were hidden panels,
offering themselves to be opened, to drink in the air.

Suddenly, the bottom of one and side of another came together
in a clasp, as if they would break loose and wander, even before
the touch of cicadas' slender sounds emerge.

So this is the way callous points of energy perform
their mysterious choreography, scribed
in wet sand until the next tongues of brine
reach forward to lick them away.

So this is the way it is going to taste,
acrid from the inside, yet with a sweet coating of
the goddesses' skin, translucent in its delicacy.

All the people now walk in a rigid line, when they
traverse the hallowed ground.

They collectively pray for the bestowal of insight,
that instead is replaced by glistening swaths
of lyrics, in a wall of captured notes.

Complacency, when looking back, becomes a thing to heal.

Cleansed, the ordinary man becomes a failing industry,
like welded sheets of steel, all that potency trembling
with the vibration of the main power source,

it's sustenance, just sufficiently, seldom completely held.

Thirsty Audience

I love stolen broken things, vaguely alive, they beg for
transformation, perhaps even life's finest costume.

Those fractured moments that others sling away,
I wear them if I can, set a new trend.

There can be harmony in squalor, love hiding in the fire of hatred.
Calm, gently overtaking haste.

Oh, the landscape that we are all familiar with can shimmer and
change, billions of pixels drifting and mixing and spilling out into
the taste buds of a thirsty audience.

I love the tendencies life invokes, and laugh when creativity
powerfully out-swims them all.

Tenderness

There can be tenderness in any moment
that enters a cloud's shadow, still tethered to the Earth,
where darkened forms carry a diary of questions,
chances to air their breath.

On a rainy day, I wipe my feet before entering someone's mind,
but there is always something missing.

The dust of imagination, the joy of time, spent.
A drop of dew in the morning, its tiny reflection
as profound as any other,
its ribbons of dazzling light, lazily flowing across my sight,

all lost without the sun.

There can be tenderness in any moment
when startled thoughts unfold, and desires' pestering
needs are seen to,

and never left behind.

The Altar

It was not Sunday,
so I looked inside a church through leaded glass.
The interior was blood red, pulsing with my halted breath.

Sunspots danced along the pews, refracted from
the polished altar where symmetry was, but had lost its
motive, as it took a jagged diversion,
midway through afternoon's sleepy corridors,
parting the branches of the aspen.

ଔ

Howland's Cove

Walk with Me

I cherish the grammar of your style,
an impeccable right, a drink of separate flavors,
where gulls discover minerals' rush to sea.

It is the uneasiness of compassion,
the fact that more will be needed, as the outside of tomorrow
becomes the inside of this chalice in time.

We are as distracted as a pair of wild geese searching for
a place to land, when we should be flying south.

Now we can fly across meridians and feel not a thing,
yet our flight is cut short by the very insight we have lost.

When men go so deeply into themselves, their vision
becomes as an arrow flies, blocked in infatuation.
Other philosophies become targets, pinned to

the slippery boundaries of infinite cold movement,
lost in time.

Walk with me, open your arms and heart with me, do not
hesitate to doubt the words of men.

Tears

Yes this winter never was a proper winter.
At times it brushed by me,
settling down in a sky somewhere else,

I don't know.

Other times I heard it moving through the trees,
with a rash of rain, and then away again, dark and silent.

Even the sweetest thoughts become tasks when
there is no one,
no one to read the array of petals, lovingly placed.

I know it is childish to shed tears,
simply because I have the urge to cry.

Fresco

Can't find the golden key wire, when copper falls
constantly in my way.

Can't ask in chanting obedience around impassioned evening girls
who discovered my modesty so that I may lament in my own
thickening anonymity.

It is as if someone were prodding exasperation, commanding it to
slide to the end of creeping vines, that cannot hold the weight.

I plunge into opacity, hoping for the wisdom I seek, where I wait, and
wait, and wait, in every passage, every mood, every language.

Whenever I make a move, a small amount of colored plaster silently
falls to the ground, from the fresco of my life.

CB

Greenwood Estuary

Sway

I sway through flesh's endless details,
affectionately flicking off dim sparks of
thoughtlessness as I go.

All along my way, these days drift by within vast, annulled visions,
set right through myriad chambers, with wolves.
and many doves, floating in flaking crimson.

So odd that blood can shed from within,

bringing the salt in my tears to merge with the salinity of northern
gales, just to form a glowing white sheen in the night,
caked along the crack in my front door.

The time exists. I know, when this man
will complete his cycle here,
and walk lightly across the sky too, with you.

Never having a trend to pitch,
never having to touch the tops of even the highest mountains,

or yearn for guiltless thoughts again.

Running Free

I say, and sometimes feel, and refrain, choosing to be
heavy with thought.

My spine, my mast, canted, contorted.

Yet before life took hold, its roots flowed straight down, nourished
with Earth's most cherished remarks.

It is early summer here in the shallows, breathing.

I wonder at all that is hidden, drunken boundaries unfastening
themselves, moving closer with each breath.

The hull that has been chosen, not by me, to make my voyage,
seems to be made of steel.

It does not flex with the storms, it remains rigid,
cold when it is cold, almost no tolerance for
the ever-changing sea.

I dreamed of running free, sails out, cutting a downwind course
into the vestibule of the cosmos.

But that would be like ushering a schoolboy into
life, before graduation.

If You Choose

The Earth here beneath my feet is scraping down,
airing her requests in wary silence.

Buds opening in the night, eaten alive by starving eyes.
Water shoaling apart, damned to fit my notion,
dragging its skin of reflection slowly through the sand.

The sea is calm today, remembering her caresses.
Nothing new will be learned in such quiet.

Only phosphorescent quelled light. lost,
stamped ever deeper, out of the grasp of temporal sight.

If you choose,

choose the dark, mysterious squid, chilled in transparency.
Acid abstinence and stillness disinfects
her moment,

as the sun sleeps.

Cleansed by the Sun

So abruptly I have come to the ending of my years,
with a drowning man's immediacy, an onlooker's constant drama.

Death will come, though,

through cities' bleached outcroppings into fields of grain
and wetlands, reaching out to the vast sea.

Healthy hearts pound like drums in cadence with the waves,
but briefly, and they be on their way,
moving always forward into the cosmos,

taking with them their sisters and brothers,
born of molten semen's flaming islands.

I have been too long here.

I move slowly up the sea-born canyon,
wavelets echoing into raven's call.

I see a small bleached shell,
its memory lost, its purpose forgotten.

Is this shell like I will be, cleansed by the sun and stillness,
protected from the shrill, nervous voices

out on the wind, searching for a place to land?

ↈ

Two Harbors, Catalina Island

February's Downpour

They recognize your pale labyrinth, looking at you, speechless,

with eyes that have little compassion,

though the deadliest burn with the smallest heat.

Could you ever draw past all this, all the pungent words

that have left you reeling, soaked in February's downpour?

It seems too simple–I know–that lovely thoughts can prevail,

putting their small gifts upon the morning,

sensing the fragrance of rebirth.

A Weathered Man

Way down the rock-faced gorge, frosted sun rings melt night's resolve,
the bay trees' glorious scent unlocked.

Astronomers should take note,
that our system of planets, our star and many moons, all revolve
around this point on Earth,

but only when need brushes the yearning within our souls.

In the realm of physics it makes no sense,
that a weathered man would come here with his daughter, as morning
sun spills across stones and water.

She says she cannot see limitations,
only opportunity.

Her mind resembles a vast plain of solar panels

feeding the dense batteries of fitful sleep surrounding her.

Yet she comes here to learn from her father's wisdom,

which—to her—resembles a familiar, fragrant candle
that has burned down, sensing cold stone where warm wax is flowing.

Tender of the Yard Hog

The fact is that I am up a tree again,
and must not deter you from feeding the wild stock.

As I line up the leaves of this rock-solid tan oak with the fast moving
clouds, I see them trembling, as in fear, or cold, or a spiritual highlight.

Yet when looking down on the back of your yard hog, knowing that his
vast and uncontrollable itch must be tended to,

I passively bow my head with the banal knowledge that
heavenly tribulation only comes to the saints,

and I can climb to the highest branches, and no more
enlightened will I be.

Bringing in of Solitude

Heavily pressed, the young friend tastes illogical markings in his ledger.
He wanted to say something, but was constantly waiting
in some sterile misfortune, with a fierce sizing of perennial shifts.

His array of harmonic intentions,
only two clicks away.

Looking to danger for festering sadness,
underneath the sheen of surface shadows,

where minute, parachuted seeds burst loose
amidst shortened breath, drifting, then touch the surface under soil
too light to drown.

His halting chapters grew narrow,
restless diction that could not keep the long pace flowing,
attempting to chamber its rounds within hollow thorns,

and beds of lichen die away.

Vessels with No Master

There is an ethereal well, its plaster chipped
to bare rock from constant use,
although many travel for days and nights, only to find it dry.

How in their primitive minds' shadows can they regard themselves as
being graceful, with the eloquence of the cosmos,

when their small vessels have no master?
They dwell within their angry choices,

unhappy in their vestibules of misguided energy,
where repetition is surely the plague of time.

When grey weather smothers our high spirits,
and galaxy's splendor is hidden, it will always be the poise we exude
as a result of our actions,

that will lead us to that ethereal well,
overflowing with healing waters and harmonic grace.

But the primitive man, living among us now
cuts his ride, slashes through anything of wonder,
cauterizes the flow of understanding.

He teaches his twisted notions,
and connects heads with tails,

so they roll through time like a giant wheel,
crushing everything with a potential for divinity.

Only those who aspire to shed instinct
and replace it with intuition, logic, and compassion,
have a way open to them, none other than that.

☙

Posada del Cortés
March 2, 2012

A Day for Prayer

The estuary has become a mirror.
It's real pretty outside, reflecting the white-spired church corridor.

Stubborn humming, born within as sunshine caresses,
stepping up to the sky.

Marvelous flesh where prayer shamelessly reshapes
curved bars of true intentions,
here upon this Northern California canvas.

With no weapons, parishioners swim like bewildered sperms, toward
billowing white clouds that change with every heartbeat.

Original Sin

I've drifted into a sepia modicum of pledging honesty.

Its underused wheels creak and skid with stiffness and wonder
at what always seems to ascend, becoming lost in obscurity.

I've tried to look into the souls of others, searching for light,
but it is their right to withhold it; I only wish to learn how to love them.

I yearn to connect with that ineffable part of them
I seldom see, or hear.

It is the days really, passing, regardless of the poignancy, or lack of it,
that unnerves me,

leaving me held motionless between the tremors of a raging world.

Shame, that the noble ones silently endure, must be the original sin,
that is passed on to us, and continues to challenge us,
seemingly without end.

Youth

I cannot say why, when you ask me why,
and I cannot simply bask in light, when there is no light.

I will not search the sky, for a ranging star,
and study the black abyss,

when only the scent of chaparral lingers in my mind, from
before, so far before.

The bouldered trails are there in the night, as they were in the day.

Every crystal of sand, every turn that led us arm in arm, tasting and
trusting what life had to give us.

We only laughed when the sun started its descent, the three of us, you,
me, and youth, a trio left to wander and wonder for a time.

Our skin was thick and tan, and the sun left only soft
blond hair upon the valleys left to taste it.

And I remember the mist in the early morning,
giving way to prodding fingers of sunlight.

I thought this would always be, I thought that there would be no
end to those glorious mornings,
with the scent of sage in your hair.

I remember gazing deep into your eyes and sensing all of the hardness of life's passage,
in a fleeting moment.

One small wafer, thin, yet boundless.

ભ

Banning House Lodge, Isthmus

Silken Specter

I see your loveliness through assorted prisms,
cool faces of the changing seasons, moving as
a silken specter, exquisite in its old work.

You are the soul's movement, with the commitment of flesh
as time will shape you.

Within you though, beauty is not a finite affair,
not a place of weather-swept end.

Your universe is full, as empty lies deep,

with shadows, clouds, and skeletal wretches
kept down by the thorny gravity that defines them.

The Thistle

The anxiety wand rises like a thistle out of a road,
through a crack in the blacktop.

Hell I've reached up through darkness too,
 into the swarming, infested air,

shown what colors I fancied I had, straight from the core of the planet,
where seeds of wisdom burn and drip like the hottest of tar.

I've boarded a sinking ship that cannot recognize her own peril,
sailing on and on, ever deeper into the waves.

ଓ

En route

In the West

Inside the sleeping city, garages wait,
dark incredible shelves, stacked with humming
chargers, playing monotone sonatas for the Mercedes
and BMWs, waiting as shackled slaves in their stalls.

For who, for what?

They wait for forward movement, and mechanical
promise.

But men are forced together, here on this planet,
in the half-light of another morning,
swinging through space, turning in a perfect template
while imperfection is their only predictable facet.

For what these men see ahead is pasture, seemingly
Infinite and abundant, a place to gather what they think
they need, and leave behind all of what they become
dissatisfied with.

For these men, who see themselves in others,
the harvest of the coming day spawns interest,
but their bones clutch the fragile nerves
that guide them,

won't let them leave now.

Why ebony and cherry wood, why not
just boards into railings, that lead away,

into the ventricles of an inspired
new existence.

Why just this diploma for a busy mind, why not
something else more noble than simple erosion,
and its weight of consequence?

Arrogance

I move warily within the shut-down factory,
bricks gaining the dust, rebar showing through
like fractured ribs.

Waves of generosity wing as doves through
broken windows, high up.

I want to take one single brick back to wherever
it was that I came from, use it to start again.

But even if I walk backwards, I never end up in
the same place.

I don't know how to be born, to live, to die.
I suppose it all comes to a person as he moves.

Seeing fast people constantly push away routes of
simple clarity evolution has wired them for,

brings tears of joy mixed with a pervasive sadness.
I didn't know there were so many languages,
arrogance spelled in so many different ways.

Existence

I went out to the woodshed to split some kindling for our fire.

I stretched my arms toward the sky, where I had seen
constellations and planets in the night.

How did this glorious morning just fix itself here,
with all of the sins that roam the world, hidden?

And just this new day, with the marvels of possibility in place,
like I prayed they would be.

All around me the small world is busy,
robins catching worms,
gophers beneath my feet digging,
and the grey squirrel,
arguing with some invisible opponent.

I dreamed last night that I could change my skin like a snake,
emerge into the day as a bright, shining object.

But I looked up at my hands, once graceful, but ungainly
now, like the branches of an old oak.

They match the life I live, riddled with objects that must be moved,
and humble ideas trundling along in disguise,
that must be picked,

like sugary apples still on the trees in late December.

Perfumed Receptacle

She came up, grateful for fresh, cold ocean currents,
holding anguish in her arms.

"I wish to be connected," she said.

"I know there is a river called corn whiskey hiding inside of you,"
I said, "but someone has built a dam across it.
Your thirst has been stifled too long here, you will have to wait,
all things must wait."

"But weeds are changing from summer brown, to green,"
she said.

"When mysteries become a source of confusion, look
for the color of the residue, look for rapids to give
way to pools of crystalline,

you must have strength to pass them by," I said.
"The dunes are constantly reshaping themselves,
so should each individual sand crystal,

your speech should be meek, as should your hands
be unrepentant."

"Yes," she said.

"A grinning spire has set its hardened root deep," I said.

"Yes, fugitive behavior has ambushed my thoughts, if only
I could cast from a different mold," she said, "but my body
has become a perfumed receptacle."

"Yet in this next second, it could change into a shrine
that would come alive, as this hapless world casts its lot,"

I said.

Isla Coronado

First it is the water, then the rock,
and then the sun that makes all things visible.

Each morning, scattered bones, desert bloom,
an island peacefully alone.

She emerges from the cool sea,
the darkest garlands, volcanic folds
give way to the persistence of life,

whose relentless features haven't forgotten
the maternal force that the deepest fires once imposed.

I can hold her in my memory, her crystal air, depth of clarity,
but when I try to describe what I have seen,

I say the words that have been said,
I speak into the dismissive pungency of man's endless rumination,

and in the evening, the island still stands,
stoic, yet vulnerable.

℃

Sea of Cortez, Loreto

Dreamers

I have wondered where things get decided.
Where clarity of thought is just a normal thing.

Can we steer our souls along and out of this geographic mire,
where mistress of equinox looks away,
where we are left with only the faint scent of tangible answers?

You speak of light and reconciliation,
then, of a future we can only imagine.
This is why you and spring flowers' brightness
and pungency have so much in common.

My reverence though, is for the celestial architects,
their wisdom gives imagination a way through.
We will follow, you and I,
dreamers in a world where dreams do not end with first light.

The Sea

If I were to draw down some breath into my open palms, where
dexterity exists, only when thrust into the domes of the sublime.

All at once, they would ignite volumes of latent
wisdom, written in a universal language.

Yet the philosopher, gathering pollen for his new discourse, must
sit amidst the trunks of a dying forest.

I grow tired of the ones who burn and glow,
but never hold the heat, cold as the wind tracing
through the eucalyptus canopy,

and on, to where the stones become submerged
and the sea resumes her endless cycle.

Casting for Graces

Every tree has its tongue in the skin of this planet,
every other moving thing does the same, in his or her own way.

Tongues are busy things, casting about for graces,
and always as mosquitoes do,
they find the pore with warm blood flowing.

Not stately as we could be, but trite.
Always covering past damage with small gifts and
repetitious repentance.

This plight is a sorry one. I bow my head with compassion for myself,
and my brothers and sisters, who take, but do not give,
talk, but do not listen.

We hasten down our paths, each with a different horizon,
with a profusion of blue-sky mornings that seem to march on
with no end.

New days with opportunities to change,
dangling like bright amulets in the sun.

ଷ

Deetjen's, Big Sur

A New Poem Is Born

I see a tree, hanging reversed.
Roots reach into the cosmos,
branches cover the skin of the Earth.

Who would believe our last days would be spent
caressing the foliage of an upside-down tree?

We are the tiny drifters now, fresh and awake,
who see with different eyes.

Now you stay, now you stray, and return back into solitude.

Each hour, a new poem is born.
Is it yours, is it mine, or does it belong to the wind?

Gathering Water

The push of gathering water can suffocate stone,
while its scythed flow slides between slenders of a bright pond.

Night has become still, glowing like a child who longs to have
her truth decide which colors to use.

In mind's open vault, we cannot wish away contenders
kneeling in pews as we pass.

Even the glowing child who has become a host for our communion
must stay corniced,
knees deep in darkened, symmetrical petals.

Dressed in Black

Here I stand alone.

Waiting seems to be a way of existence for me.
Charms and banishments all roll into a large
staging area, in a central plaza, somewhere.

Its address printed on placards moving toward indifferent locations,
never within the perimeter of my sight.

I dressed in black today, it becomes the contour of my body, I think,
yet it also becomes a magnet, rounding up light-colored objects.

I watch them.

They could be souls, drifting, magnetized, as the dark world beckons,
seeking solace in the one thing intangibly attractive to them.

Just as they seem to be, I have become,
predictably relenting to the lure of generosity.

Yet, many of life's generalities regarding human behavior,
depend on a symmetry of wings, so that we will not fly in circles.

ଓ

Moody's

Into the Mist

Little tufts of grass sprout along the malecón,
lifting broken shards of concrete
like newly-born stepping stones with no direction.

A man picks his way through,
glancing at the barren islands just offshore.

A woman sits in the shade of a fast-moving cloud,
pretending she isn't interested in anything.

A gull with strange markings follows the contours north,
into a mist and a bluish hedge of dunes.

॰

Laredo, Baja

The Navigator

My weakened self
will not acquiesce to the specter with the broken wing,
whose eyes can swim disabled,
but still move throughout the passages.

Every person is master of his own ship.
Measurement brings depth, and passage under
the stars brings conviction.

I imagine someone listening, crying with us,
a navigator fragile with compassion.

I imagine listening to him, to her, listening to her gift of guidance,
suspending my power of choice for something with
a catalyst far too far to reach.

Landing Crystal

Fallen Leaf Lake curls up to fit inside unrelenting granite.
Purer water, I never have felt.

Summer seldom comes, and spring is always nudging winter.

This lake so blue, has become a landing crystal.

Wild berries count how hard a vision blood runs through.

Beings that have a destructive edge,
never find the humble turnoff, never get to see another's heaven.

Visitors from other worlds come crashing into the lake at night.

The great splashes form a cadence,
that embrace my thoughts, and soothe me to sleep.

Begging Bowl

All the Earth speaks the same language,
and pours her notes into the same begging bowl.

As the bowl overflows,
small paper butterflies spill into a raging sky.

Some ask for brevity and peace.
Some turn every change with poise,
and wish for more.

Cotton Lake

As I approached a small dock on Cotton Lake,
it floated away into a deeper future, into mist
and unused time.

Impulsively, I built another, softening boards
that covet a home in the shallows.

Hedonistic crowds emerge into a collective howl, moving into simple
gestures wearing their inevitable masks.

Still, nothing to tie to, but your voice as it leans precariously.

Do you hear me as I work the keys, open sacred doors,
become alone again, even as you tell me your confluence of
living within an open wound?

Time

Measured depth records her name with all revelations, fans
her script on a pike for all to taste, and then swiftly
ledgers life's whisper in trembling haste.

She races in, astride a certain trance, riding frigid rails north of chords
of green. Her name can bring harmony where swamps have drained
and become lovely gardens, and her friends who make no journeys
watch her comet's blurry trail.

I love to pick iris in late winter, and trade only subtle thoughts,
and watch time in her broad reach cut across the sky.
Yet I am left with only passage when looking back,

time that has been traversed,

only that.

Carefully Lost

Your scent is what is left after thrill subsides.
Burning low,
it is the embers that I find myself coiling among.

Carefully lost, whispering heat, disregarding ebony boundaries.

I play gently through the seasons here,
never letting strangers in.

Sewn tightly the flesh of my resolve,
sutures pull, but seldom break.

Starships

Together, together, together, yet apart as we ever shall be.

Starships suspended in time,
claiming such velocity, yet not moving,
only picture-still,

valiantly searching for the power we know exists.

We canonize those mysterious ones
who claim to have deciphered resonating factors
that follow a source of light,
too high above our mineral-rich surface,

too far for our telescopes to reach.

If I Knew

If my heart would fit inside a shell,
worn like a hermit crab,
I could go on wandering this blue orb, unafraid, unharmed.

I could take my sorrow straight up, like the man I know I could be.

If I knew my life wasn't hanging on a rusty hinge,
I could swim and dive, love and sin.

I could stand on the rim of heaven,

looking in.

CB

Library at Deetjen's

Ferns

The collaboration of light upon light upon light,
coursing through twin gorges—faith and grace—

will still not surrender to the fabric of the misty human mind.

Even though you may have many eyes, yet fail to hear that
crashing sound, just beyond the salted blissful night sky.

When ruin has all its edges up, all raised and sharpened harm,

I shall be a child of the curious, even though I belong to
the family of sin, disillusioned by the works of men.

Have you noticed how ferns always thrive in
the most beautiful places?

They are like divine punctuation in a perennial prayer.

I vow to be like them.

ଓଃ

Botanical Gardens

The Gift of Pain

When I think of the weight of consequence,
I feel burden saturating the capillaries of my existence.

I can see out of the darkness, only through vertical fissures
in the unknown substance that holds ethereal staves in place.

Through them, the colorless wind brings us
the gift of pain.

Without it, we will not know ourselves, or the ones we say we love.

Where We Used to Be

Happiness rained down on us when you were here,
like drops of honey from the sky.

Never mind those words of mine that sent you away.

Under its wing, a loose feather flies in the wind,
on up the mountain, chasing shadows, never reaching the top.

My journey has left me with nothing but grains of sand in my pockets,
memories of you sifting through the old cloth of my life.

I can stand and look down on the ones who will follow, their eyes
as clear as truth,

but moths fly about inside of my head,
and cold fingers are touching the back of my arms.

Thoughts of honey in my tea, in a place where the wind does not blow.
Shame is just a word,
if I could go back, I think that I would.

Youth is where we used to be, a place to visit, but never return.

Tactics

Walking and talking with friends.
Not to step into that toxic pool of controversy
becomes a tightrope affair,

that can drag its bloated mound of feathers,
up just to the height of where we breathe,
smothering us into a bracketed sameness.

I look around and see bodies postured for a fight,
yet there is no fight.

In sleep, potential combatants read tactics on the inside of
their eyelids, so when they confront a new day,
they will know what not to say.

Universal Mother

There is a place on the bow of the schooner
where the teak has been rubbed into a sheen.

The dolphins occasionally look up,
and sense the earthbound poets and philosophers
who have pondered the cosmos there.

They caress her hull like their universal mother.

If the ocean didn't love her, surely she would
sink into the depths, like something worthless and dark,

cast off from mysterious lands
that hold the water in.

℃3

Nepenthe

Pride

It's so hard for me to know where you start, and where you end.
You shade my comprehension,

amplify my voice by your heart-pounding entrance,
born not of flesh's mottled way.

You embrace like a dam with nothing to hold.
You sense my hesitation, then laugh, clinging to me.

The Journey

Upon awakening, the landscape of mind comes into a halo of second
light, and here again we measure, crossing dust with
an unfamiliar glare.

Memory blooms, sweeping forgotten rooms, I shall wait for you there.
I have grown and prospered, yet I am still just a boy, my face turning
away from harsh answers.

Quite cold is a life meant to be lived where wind falls, where the most
powerful words become prayers.

Where we journey for days, for weeks, never reaching the sea.
Yet I am bound to all of this, as a man who owes a cleft in his heart
as ransom for clarity in his mind.

My shortened breath shifts as rain fills shallow ponds white silence,
feelings begin to fray, to shatter,

finding me letting go of my ferocity for living, yet loving the litany,
loving the Quetzal for his magnificent plumage, thirsting
for the caress of the angels.

I cannot hold a lifetime of work in the small of my hand.

It takes a body, enshrouded within it's divine soul, breathlessly
beautiful, as it enters the softest shores, to joy's purest flow, where it
rains with the grace of heaven, to hold spiritual excellence.

To earn our God's knowledge, we must stay, learn, transform if we can.

The Gate

Here in the coveted meadow, here the terminal
butterflies dangle like mummified amulets.

Here, I was the water carrier held breathless at the gate,
just as any water criminal would be.

Here, thick, silver clouds rushed at me, pounding me with
the notion of a never ending cycle, smashing
beaches into ever-finer sand crystals.

Here at the gate, I will leave forever the ones my parents would have
been proud of,

legions of glow worms, seduced by chance, but never leaving their bodies.

Here I will wait for a tomorrow that may be skidding through time,
never aware of a small portal, trespassing in its vast stillness.

Visitors

This equatorial sun wants to burn me, tattoo
its image on my shoulder.

Beings from a neighboring solar system have
completed their assimilation, wrapped in black velvet.

Their arrival becomes lighter than air, strange
in its familiarity.

What would happen to the edge of sound,
receding thunder from a passing tempest,
whose axe against a tender breast

would love to crack a gash in waxing splendor?

What would happen if the fog became so thick
that we would change, even the way we
became enraged, even to the end, perhaps?

I tug at something soft and dark, abandoned
space veils, carefully folded, merging with
absence.

I am still not afraid, as love and fear entwine,
strike at all that has become irrelevant,
leaving but few glowing paths,

guided by the touch of what we vow to be,
not what we have become.

The songs of men fall short when distance prevails,
like all else, the subject at hand.

Wavelets softly breaking in the sand.

There is no escape, except death's rolling thunder
on the horizon, and the perfect breath of
the angels.

www.ingramcontent.com/pod-product-compliance
Lightning Source LLC
LaVergne TN
LVHW041229080426
835508LV00011B/1118